Bitter Matriarch

Poems on Family, the Universe and Belonging

Rebecca Trowbridge

Copyright 2019 by Rebecca Trowbridge. All rights reserved.

No portion of this book may be reproduced or transmitted in any form or by any means, electronic or mechanical, including photocopying, recording, or by any information storage and retrieval system without written permission from the author.

This book contains emotional micro-memoirs and meditation journeys. It reflects the author's present recollections of emotional experiences over time. Names and characteristics have been changed, events compressed, and dialogue recreated.

"Dead Mosquito" by Arthur Costil used under CC BY-SA 3.0 (https://creativecommons.org/licenses/by-sa/3.0/deed.en) by Rebecca Trowbridge. Contrast increased from the original (located at https://commons.wikimedia.org/wiki/File:Moustique_écrasé.jpg).

Acknowledgements

Dear E and *david is goliath* were previously published in The Enchanting Verses Literary Review (Australian Edition) 2019.

The Middle Path and other stories in this book came from merged visions in personal meditations. The final line of *Letting Go of Dad* is from Karen McRae's *Are You There?*

This book could not exist without the experience of meditating with Loreto Whitney and fellow regular meditators—Catherine McCormack, Laney Kauter, Waeger sisters Karin and Hella, Emma Digance, Lyn Hartigan, Lyn Tucker, April Young, Nikki Borgelt—your insights helped me become a better human with something to write about. As for becoming a better writer (and also human) I thank members of writers' groups (such as Hunter Writer's Centre) for editing these pieces, especially regular editors April Klasen, Nicole Sellers, Phil Williams, Deb Arthurs, Diana Pearce, Trisha Green, Naomi Johnson, Ellen Shelley, Bron MacRitchie, Maxine Jacobi, Megan Buxton, Karen Crofts and Cassandra O'Loughlin.

Thank you, Kelly Alfris and Claire Parkes, for your very much appreciated reader feedback. Thank you to my partner Nigel and my two wonderful girls for their love and presence, and to the parental figures in my life for their teachings. Some conversations sparked my muse—thank you to Heather Stevens, Myffawny Lawrie, Lou-Anne Page, Agnetha Mitchell, Joanne Nelson, Trevor Howells, Natalie Lunn, Eunha Joung, Shashona McCall, Krista Imberger, Whitney Martin and Ann Harrison.

Author Biography

Rebecca Trowbridge currently juggles high school teaching, family and writing. She has spent time as an army corporal, geologist, market research caller, ski lodge manager and university tutor, while living and working around Australia from the outback to the coast. She has a Masters in Volcanology and wants you to know that lava flows downhill. Her other books, for young people, are:

- Cherry Chicken Chocolate Kitchen
- Congraduations! You Finished!
- Fond Farewells: Stories that Comfort when Saying Goodbye

Contents

Parent/Child

My Mother Had Me Tortured & Killed in Shang Times 9

    ii. But We've All Done That 9

    iii. Emperor of China 10

Curses 12

Zen Enough 14

Unsung Rhizome 16

The Middle Path 18

Adopted for Two Hours 20

Kryptonite 22

    ii. Cryptogenic 22

Bitter Matriarch 24

Reflux 26

Growth

Three Turn Up to Meditation 28

Iiyama 31

A Firm Hand 35

    ii. Attitude Adjustment 37

Stinging-Tree Wisdom 39

Defining Schadenfreude 40

ii. Clarification 42

Moon Moves On 43

david is goliath 47

Awakening Ghazal 48

The Third Mirror 50

Belonging

Dear E 52

Graphology 55

Merlin's Owl 56

How Can I Belong Anywhere 57

Tentacles 59

After We Cleaved 62

Superpower 63

Black Sheep Ballade 64

Table 66
    ii. Children 66
    iii. Homestay 67
    iv. Relativity 68
    v. Pleasure 69

Naga Uta: Observance 70

Thank you, Softball Dad 71

Approximate Pentina 72

Andromeda 74

Embracing Life after Four Months of Bronchitis 77

Waiting 78

Letting Go of Dad 80
    ii. An Old Haunt 82
    iii. Three's a-Proud 82

Rebirth 84

Parent/Child

My Mother Had Me Tortured & Killed in Shang Times

Here I
        still in her face be-
        headed I
stand again.

We stub-
        born, die for three-and-a-bit millennia
arguing like idiots.

ii. But We've All Done That

O, tremendous. Am I
        the righteous vind-ictim of
that blinded, bitter, stony, battle-axe
reflection?

3000 years clean-handed?
That likeliness is
extremely
small
.

iii. Emperor of China

She was

of the Shang dynasty.
That one insight
by the wise-woman
explained our life.

She is tickled,
booking restaurants as
Emperor of China
with her pal
Princess of Tonga.

They are the centre of merriment
at yum cha
fêted by the maître
d' and waiters.

Do I tell her the Emperor
executed a friend
for defending a peasant
blamed for a flood?

Best not dredge that up.

We have plenty on our plates

at present.

Curses

You'll fall, Grandma warns
kids climbing the counter.
Confess a crime and some friend
reminds you of karma.

We curse ourselves, curating words
serving self-hate at worst
or else clouting authority
like a doctor's prognosis.

"You better start doing things for yourself,"
I say to my seven-year-old,
"like me at your age
when my dad died."

I am upstanding, proctoring
Self-Reliance in a shortcut;
Gratitude without the grieving
like the trope about
walking uphill 100 miles to school barefoot in the snow
swayback in the day.

I imply she must prove herself,
as if she isn't wonderful,
and do things the hard way for the dubious moral fibre
stemmed up my rectum.
I am an icon, stipitate,
nobly cursing her seventh birthday
hence ourselves to repeat past events;
laying sin on the subconscious of the next generation.
My love is anxiety
boding doom, binding
her into ill-suited stories.

For a whole year
her dad wakes, glad he is alive
due to fear of dropping dead
as if I would rather be right than happy.

She turns eight,
the curse lifts.
Her birthday gift:
Mum's smothered tongue.

Zen Enough

She can make her own toast
fill a kettle on tiptoes,
boil it.
Then I'll serve the noodles
but today, in secret, she manages
to scald herself with a brimming bowl.

After first aid, sympathy-face and hugs,
we work out the error of her way
to the table: focused on her instant reward
rather than every step forward
tending the tideline between her palms.
Slow Down is our old strain
that tripped on information gaps
because today she asks, welted,
How do I slow down?

I confess I stopped
over-tipping jugs
to hurry water into a glass.
I now watch the spout
for pouring's procession

while the glass seems to fill itself
in one expanded moment.

I compare the ages
I gained patience
and this child gets it in ten minutes
because I, the alleged teacher,
earned patience by her

though I've thought otherwise:
witnessing my tantrums
occasioning change.

I don't have the patience of angels,
but if I can teach a little
then I am patient enough
for Earth, for now.

Unsung Rhizome

When will I find an illustration,
without the inscrutable pond,
of the lotus with its loot
which is just as lotus yet

plainly deemed graceless?
Maybe nobody wants to view
parasols impaling pinched stools
or large-skirted ladies in a sinking boat.

Or maybe the best part is cloaked
for the boon that it is
by petal-lashed periscopes
guarding the handgrip;

by florid-faced sailors
stockpiling sausages;
by sleights of bloom
concealing the root

of all crispy, fried, thin-sliced crunch;
of sappy strings from thick cuts

boiled in salty pea soup;
al dente, with some coconut punch.

How do they taste this good
despite murky water and mud?
Chopping will tell you:
in cross-section, tubes

funnel and filter
the useful in darkness
to anchor bright blossoms
with quiet, distilled wisdom.

The Middle Path

"Mummy why are they different?"

We walk along the narrow, serrated ridge separating the two sides of the island. Puffing, I flick a hand to the jungle's rising cool. "Mountain catches clouds this side. All rain falls there." I twitch an arm to the barren west. "Black rock absorbs sun. Burns everything."

"Is the black rock bad?"

I prop a foot on a boulder, pausing. "It's all over the island, sweetie. It's called basalt, from lava flows, from deep in the earth. It's so rich you can grow babies in it. This side holds the heat, though. Kills anything off that takes root. Things get a chance to grow on the wet side."

"Mummy, can we rest?"

Oh, hell yeah. We sit, legs dangling on the licorice side of Pele's brow. Ropey basalt plaits the goddess' midnight hair from our ridge down to the spray-topped turquoise of the west coast, as the beauty emerges for breath, in perpetuity.

"Mummy, I'm hungry."

We scratch mozzie bites, scanning over our shoulders for a food source in the dense green wall. "I think there's mango over there."
"Can you gediit?"
Her nasal whine triggers my intolerance. The umbra of the inner patriarch.
"If I go by myself, I eat all mangos by myself. You want it, you earn it."
"Mummyyy…!" But Mummy is spent, and only Daddy is here. Daddy is focussed on this Crosscut Saw, where the kid had to get comfortable with both sides. The only way was through. No short-cuts. No free rides.

We spend hours clambering off the path, bush-bashing to a mango tree, negotiating thorns, mini-beasties and the obstacle course engineered by an enmeshing undergrowth. She enjoys the canopy, mangoes and adventure, but we emerge in relief for the west's broad black desert. We breathe deeper, as permitted by the bigger vista. It is easier to see choices here. The water is jewelled and irresistible to the dipping sun, shaking out coral pinks, blush and purple onto our boat moored hours below.

Adopted for Two Hours

I can't answer the leathery wavy-haired lady
fast enough. I prattle,
glad for the company
as she probes:
Where am I going? What are my plans?
Where is my family? How old am I?

then prompts herself:
"My teens must wonder where I am."

"Oh," I say, "You should go home then.
It was lovely to meet you!"

She surveys the deserting sun
soaking red her dusty bare town
and a single rucksack;
the bus-sign stalk's shadow
fingers drinkers dekameters away.

"No, I'll stay."

An hour later I board the next leg,
hug cheerio to that mama from Kunanurra,

never thinking until 24 years later
of the grace she gave:

to meet at 42, myself—
an excited, gushing, young person
in that memory. Her kind guardianship held
not a word to disabuse me
of my faith in people.

Kryptonite

This droning buzz downs me;
the signal nonsensical:

blight noise as blowflies rebound in the skull.
Blitzed, thoughts scatter. I autopilot, hazed;

a zombie reaching for a better waltz
but beat, arms drudge, lack joy.

Where is the clear space above this electron fog?
I scrape and dent and draining interblearance remains.

Where is the mind-balm my daughter applies?
My mother arrived with the oop-osite effect.

ii. Cryptogenic

I ask to lift this oppressive depression:
revealed as the weight of the word

Unloveable.

Anything for levity:
prayer, meditation, YouTube;

I succumb to pills, private space, sleep
then scrabble in the mixed bag

of decisions, recollections
confirming community and children contradict

Unloveable.

Dreams inform me of foreign morale
usurping my centre. Whose is this

Unloveable?

Though crippling my limbs,
invading my lymphs, it is not mine

but an intergenerational belief:
Mother's miasma, inherited,

seeks a new host—until I,
by decryption, dissolve the geist.

Bitter Matriarch

Gloomy resentment is duly disguised:
duty robs freedom but praise is the prize;
service is purpose is worth, she was taught.
Smiling, her smile does not meet her eyes.

Family saps her, the amber has dried.
She's the tree's jewel when her role's fossilized:
Pleaser Entrapped, obligated and caught;
gloomy resentment is duly disguised.

Your lot might blossom—she inwardly cries
with sour regret for each self-compromise
caring too much about what others thought—
smiling, her smile does not meet her eyes.

Someone must pay for a life misapplied:
do not presume you can ripen and thrive.
You will stay small with her malcontent sort;
gloomy resentment is duly disguised.

She is a warning to choose otherwise;
this bitter blaming you'll see calcify.

Thank her in spirit for lessons hard-bought,
(smiling, her smile does not meet her eyes)

counselling courage to live as you like.
Fear, doubt and danger she'll proselytize
fatally living as she Should and Ought:
gloomy resentment is duly disguised,
smiling, her smile does not meet her eyes.

Reflux

Dump your vitriol, unrefined,
into your child
to grow a malevolent
adaptive contempt.

You—sixty-seven
declining, softened—
wince when he rolls that acid barrel down
to your grandchild.

Touch your son's arm, murmur in his ear
that you are here for him, always
but a caustic history
corrodes this late crooning.

Now pander to your hand-fed Hyde,
your expanding hydra,
and, shrinking by your shadow,
pray it doesn't savage you
like it has everyone else.

Growth

Three Turn Up to Meditation

The other two are mediums.
One communes with Aboriginal Elders. When she is
ready, a spirit from her line will speak through her.
One is 85, Welsh, and channels the Chinese Goddess
Kwan Yin.
I am thrilled and honoured to do circle work with these
spiritually advanced, then surprised the night turns to
challenges with money.

"I thought money was a white man's curse:
as soon as we got it, we had to spend it straightaway
because it is evil
and no one in my family wants to touch it.
And it was never our culture to have money
but these whitefellas hand out the money
and neither we nor they understand how it fixes anything.
If you want to give my family anything,
give us food!
We know what to do with food.
But lately I'm learning to save a little bit
and it's there when I really need it."

"Well, I grew up in the Depression

and we were never "poor"; there was no "poverty";

we all bought "on tick"; we all had the same background.

Nonetheless, I did always seem to

not be able to pay bills,

and I once owed three thousand dollars

and it may as well have been three million

but I am an honest person and I was going to pay the bill.

I called the company and spoke to a nice lady

who asked a lot of questions.

After 15 minutes, she told me she'd cancelled it,

a kindness that affects me still.

Yet what did I say?

"NO, I'll Pay It Back!"

But she'd forgiven the debt already."

I share

that during the Chinese Cultural Revolution

—where any educated or wealthy or even wore glasses

were sent to work the fields

or worse

because none better be better than anyone else—

my family hid their prosperity

until someone turned fink and the family fled

to Hong Kong, then the U.S. or Australia to live low-key.

"Mum thinks acting poor is how she keeps money

—a bag-lady mentality—

as wealth is an invitation to persecution.

I mortgaged all my money, hoping to remove the jinx.

People took my energy instead,

which I now value more,

and I learned to guard both, to survive."

We bring down the light, merge into All That Is,

receive from the One-ness

then flow into the eucalypt night

with a cleaner economic understanding.

Iiyama

We disembark the suburban train onto the open platform, where frost paces impatiently for trains that are never late. The Iiyama landscape is a white, hushed spell with a rail line scar etched as if for a magical marble carving. We proceed toward escalators; in the sheltered lower station a hot 7-11 coffee awaits my claim.

The air BAWLs, pitching me toward a banister; old army training insists I go to ground. A bullet train storms the platform, blasting air at such fury that I am strafed by its thunder, before it slows, snaking to rest.
My God, this one is ours. My family get on with finding seats. I find a friend on the platform before time propels the train.
"Hello!" She greets my face with relief. "You're catching this one?"
"Yes. You coming?"
Her brow furrows; darkened eyes dart to the carriage, then to the stark platform, then to the crowd going below for comfort. She could also go below, or board, or she could stand in limbo here— understandably intimidated.

We look up at icicles glittering along and between the snow-sculpted trees. Flitting at the peaks are wispy smoke spirits, each one a long, twitchy curl of sooty vapor. They swirl at the top of telephone poles, or daring, rest flickering flame-like at the proximate roof of this platform. They are only noticeable to the informed as a fleeting movement in the peripheral vision, while they shadow the station for the right host to jump into. What does Eckhart Tolle say? Life is the dancer and we are the dance. If she can handle this winter, she'll be ok. If she can't, she won't stay herself if she remains here—to become lost and bedevilled.

"I have to go… please get on a train…? I know change is hard. Even if you go alone, you can still send for your family once you get there. If they want to come."
Even I am unconvinced of my decision. If not for my family I would baulk too. The train points further north and there is nothing about the platform, the train's arrival and the chill that promises anything better than risking the smoke spirits to stay below with other refugees and coffee's comfortable bitterness.

Inside the carriage, which is surprisingly warm—half-full in a consoling, respectful companionship—I see her right outside my window. My eyes plead with hers, a mix of sorrow and compassion that she is alone on that platform. She has choices yet to make, but I have no assurances.

The train leaves with its usual consternation, though inside is a soft buzz, cheered by the fascinating refreshment trolley calling down the aisle. Marble thickens outside, casting trees as snow-monsters while daylight dwindles to grey and a light haze of whirling snow camouflages any monkeying smoke spirits.

Unexpectedly, other panoramas flash by the windows: the grey-tossed Japan sea magnified to discern each white-cap; the perching, dense city-scape of Shin-Osaka; the fluorescent, colour-burst paradise of Tokyo subways; the placid, sunny quietude of Yokohama jetties. I decide on the latter but on stepping off I perceive a vacuum—the air stilled. There is no Life here. A good place to convalesce, but there is nothing to learn here other than observe my own projections, again. The kids were right: back to Tokyo, but I warn them we will eventually move to the famed western-most islands.

And I have seen enough to tell my friend:

that she's not alone;

that she needn't stop at North;

that there's better waiting for her than where she is;

that the unknown is an adventure;

that the platform is for efficient transfer than lingering;

that the roar of the train is the roar of life

and like Warriors we have to say YES

(though the train is just fine inside)

if she just moves forward, trusting she is the right track.

A Firm Hand

When I thirst for beer—
did I tap into *your* corked craving?
Did an earth-trapped spirit stick to me?
Am I coping with echoes on my emotional calendar?
Or was an alcoholic past life—some story in the ether—
triggered today?

First response: direct whatever-it-is to the light
then imagine colour cleanse my body
to be myself again
though if I deduce what this odd mood is
it will d i s s i p a t e
teaching empathy and
                        release.

That's how I maintain boundaries
to navigate the nebulous
energy soup we swim in.

In the meantime
I say to those ancestors, guides and angels

   respecting free will, sending signs;
   the Light-Dwellers, the Infinite:
Thank You for your Presence
but do be sure
   as I scurry to the toilet in the wee hours
not to show yourselves,
so I don't shit myself.

I remember that time
I glimpsed an outline in the doorway
and I bucked
   then berated whoever you were
   four-greats-grand-aunt whatsername,
   that I am Not Impressed
   since *I* am in the physical and not about to
   humour your antics like oldies on Contiki tours
   expecting young'uns to carry their bags.
   If you want to manifest then go and get born
   and have a body to do whatever.
   Just because you're my ancestor
   doesn't mean you get to be in my face.
   I have children to do that
   and a mother who thinks I'm still a teenager
   which may be true but you stay out of it.

All I ask is just ONE thing
        and something couldn't help itself.
        I didn't know which, so you were all ignored
        and while that may hurt me
        it is part of teaching discipline
        because even the afterlife is working things out.

They know I am all bluff
trying to outrun the dark.

I know they love me
I've not seen them since.

ii. Attitude Adjustment

They show me love
with a nightmare intervention:

She stares at my friend,
absorbing his soul.
At my window: a doll
then two, with his face and mine;
black wings swirl by.

A green grinning man at that window says
"Let me in", tap tap, "Let me in", grin grin.

I wake, aware
of the message:

don't call that lady.
You can't handle it.
You are now warned
for your psychic protection.

I wake, humble
with close-call gratitude
and maturing to do.

Stinging-Tree Wisdom

Rainforest ambush

or river sentry,

armed with green

hair-trigger hearts:

light-pocked leaves

flag our rash charge,

invite, instead,

a circumspect tread.

Gympie bristles serve

fines for lack of care

of self, scrub and sphere.

Every warning is a boundary:

Disrespect begets

terrible regret.

Defining Schadenfreude

It is: vindication when your mother is disappointed by a favorite child.

It is not: personal validation or sky-thrilling freedom from a) any negative self-view arisen from old family dynamics and b) your mother's conversations about him.

It is: glorying in another hiking group's complaints of an over-chatty member on a two-day camping trip because it means your group had a better time and therefore you are winning.

It is not: relief that you did not spend 48 hours with that person; gratitude towards your own hiking group for their wonderful company.

It is: delight at the struggles of a daughter-in-law who stole your son and has girl-children you covet; stony satisfaction in shared misery.

It is not: smiling at someone's struggles because you relate to their vulnerability. You know this experience will make them a fearless and happier person, gaining inner strength just as you did.

It is: enjoying the misfortune of anyone you hate; enjoying that anyone is hated.

It is not: laughing at slapstick-like accidents whether or not you apologise for laughing; black humour that has evolved from a shared knowledge of life's grimness.

Uses: awareness that success can attract schadenfreude; knowledge of your own schadenfreude will keep you from hubris. Congratulations on your schadenfreude.

Contra-indications: self-combustion in demoniacal ecstasy.

ii. Clarification

When my rival's ruination holds a gleeful fascination:
Schadenfreude sh sh schadenfreude sh sh!

When I need my peers to fail as validation I prevail:
Schadenfreude sh sh and competition tsk tsk!

Blaming someone else means the bully is yourself:
Merely malice tut tut merely malice tut tut!

Minding my contentment? Nah! Rejoicing in resentment!
Stubborn rancor tsk tsk stubborn rancor tsk tsk!

A foe's upset enthralls for its rare karmic windfall:
Schadenfreude sh sh schadenfreude sh sh!

Moon Moves On

Light washes through me. I bleach: hair blanches silver; freckles decolour; brown eyes fade green, blue then white; bones fluoresce through skin. I lift into the atmosphere, rolling upward. I am a white ball spiralling over an arcade Moon. I spin into a focal funnel, rifling until the tunnel's end in the central system.

A deep sigh vibrates the wall curved on my back. More vibrations transmute into words, through the medium of my flesh. "You're in the way."
Ah. The tunnel's view is of Earth.
"Oh! I beg your pardon. You've been watching Earth?"
Will the celestial Moon—solace to all who witness night, the hypno-tidal Great Stone Face—make small talk?
"So...how do you feel when you look at the Earth?"

"Oh, Earth is so beautiful. I am so proud of Earth's beauty. In the meantime, I just try to take in every angle and remember every surface, since I won't have this view forever."

I recall from Geology 101 that Moon, after sweeping orbital debris into self-aggregation, had been so close to Earth that the global tides were 20 metres high, scraping nutrients from rock, to furnish life. Passions cooled as those very tides worked to slow Earth's rotation and the difference in momentum transferred to enlarging Moon's orbit. They were drifting apart. The longest breakup in deep time.

"I see. And… does Earth love you?"
"Of course."
Silly question. They are two great friends circling each other in admiration.
"It must feel bittersweet", I say.
"Yes. But it's fine, really. I do so love the quiet. I really do enjoy the ways things are, actually."
"Ah, 'honouring the journey', and all that, I suppose."
We are hanging in space, so peaceful. Moon's pale, open face is unblinking as ever. Our words echo down the tunnel to puncture the infinite silence outside.
"Well, I've got to this point where my path is clear and calm. And Earth has blossomed so much since the tides calmed down. Since I...stepped back."
"But you want One-ness? And you don't want to ruin

everything?"

In answer, Moon sighs, preoccupied with Earth.

The distance, the circumspection, the phases of shyness now make sense. All the work done, Moon only had to let go. When would Moon ever think it was ready? I need air. I am cramped, tucked here with a single remote view, eons yawning. My heart hammers at the confinement, curled as I am, a sphere within a sphere, a fetus fomenting escape. I breathe hard, try to shift my shoulders or kick, anything to let the steam off this terrible, surging agitation.

KABLOOEY!

I stretch into giant cosmic form, shattering Moon to gather all fragments and crush them to dust that sprinkles from my hands into Earth's biosphere. Like a toddler smashing block-stacks, I am exultantly free. I grin mischief with a clever solution.

Shoots emerge from the soil. I shrink for a closer look. Petals unfurl into white crocus towers and I step amongst the stems, slanting a smiling glance under a low-perched hat-brim at marvelling visitors. My dust-caked boots and worker khakis hide this garden's secret bubbling glee within me.

Moon had no need to despair. The two are just gorgeous together.

david is goliath

children dive-bomb a crocodile
catfish swallow corpses

hairy caterpillars—
scalp collectors—
skeletonize gums

banyan leaves rasp
eardrum-drilling
psithurism

mosquitoes bring death
more than any other creature

Awakening Ghazal

I'm dammed behind certainty. Science has girt me.
No access for diverse beliefs to subvert me.

You're Mormon? Jehovah? Or some church uniting?
I'm guarded in small talk in case you'll convert me.

Dissatisfied thirties: the spirit gets thirsty,
means sating this vessel. First empty, invert me.

No group's persecuted in name of The Oneness?
Astrology? New Age? Tarot shouldn't hurt me?

Self-truth is a lone wolf yet Seeking's real teacher
for gurus change ways and at times disconcert me.

Dysfunction's transmuted by unexplained healing:
shamanically-roused strength I win won't desert me.

I'm trying new language, the cosmos converses
(attention's important). I let it alert me.

Appraising the signs that the universe brings is
seduction by mirror-talk. O, reassert me!

No wonder believers think theirs is a true faith:
this God speaks my babble; affirms what I blurt: Me.

I worry about the forgetting of godhood
but One swears more learning means life can't revert me.

While merging to wholeness, the work is a circle:
we teach what we most need to learn. Yes! Exert me!

The Third Mirror

of the Essenes

Something I lost
inhabits my yearning:
an upturned face,
a creative blur.
A spark I crave
meets me at depths
where grief echoes love echoes home.

                    I trudge this traverse,
              long for the marvels I've seen in you
           but seeing means I embody them too:
                        You twin light
                        I can salvage
                        within; recoup
                    a forgotten virtue.

        Wholeness returns
        and aching adjourns.

Belonging

Dear E

You claimed problems with language, imagined flaws in vocality: mute in a miserable job, stung, tied in self-blame. We sought silver in the panning. "That's the shot," your partner says, "positive bloody thinking." But your toddler's shrieks were revelations in clear meaning. You spoke up at work and the changes came home, threatening your partner. We didn't realise, when you took ownership of your self, the trespass on territory marked for his kin:

your real job is to fit in; you're in our town now darl; best practice your English because we don't need to make an effort to understand; why can't you make your point like this or that so we can pretend not to hear however you twist your tongue; we'll just ignore you because Asian girls are supposed to look after their elders and respect only goes one way in this rural town; there's a pecking order of conditional love and you're at the bottom in case you haven't worked it out by the way we casually disregard your feelings,

your thoughts,

your wishes,

your hopes.

Dear E,

We discovered our insecurities were collateral for in-laws to short the change they need. Yours encamped to crowd your fire and betrayed their long shadows. They were so close, entitled, reducing you to a flicker; an ember lacking air. I am deeply sorry for my arrogance, pushing positivity, showing off my rude coping, patronizing our feelings which did not need fixing.

>> The truth is you speak and our stories cohere.

I asked my partner: were you were raised by a single parent? I was. I know what to expect—a rocky bed—but I arose to grow flowers better than I was shown. I do not worry about my girls: we can survive you and these people; we'll transplant from this noxious hometown. The history that hurt me is now grounds for my strength: an utter faith I earned in myself as the mother bear I've yearned for and learned I've become.

His family tree feeds on blood and validation. To germinate new growth, let's burn these old structures with easy rage—awakened from ringed helplessness—for the stand in our authority is the same whether to an audience of one or many.

Let's relinquish the rosy outlook, martyr making the best of things, to recognize our grit. I am proud of you E; I am proud of my mother, of us. I am proud of our partners who chose rebirth as their own live young—the future. Our mettle scores our full chests and freedom.

Graphology*

is black-art analysis
to spot on the page
a lie or rage or shame
channelled as muscles twitch
marking truth
whatever the words.

My old signature riddles
with loops of pretense.
I stare at the blot;
I lament for the girl
in hiding.

The study of handwriting regarded as an expression of the writer's character and emotions.

Merlin's Owl

The table bears scales, herbs, stones, a book open at a spell, an owl with no propriety but the good taste to share the coherent confusion for it accepts an offered mouse then noiseless, wings to the window. "How has this cut berry purpled?" Merlin murmurs to his gorging friend. "There could be value in the study." He accepts the rip of flesh by rivetted claw and beak as wisdom: they spell utensil, which Merlin inspects. The bird shits and leaves, a share of mouse tail for its fascinating human. They have an agreement—the other is a friend: free, not a pet. "My thanks"; Merlin scrapes the droppings for an unguent, plucks the tail for a spell—a cure for loneliness, perhaps. He is as unique and therefore alone as anybody else—he knows that healing accepts weakness, sensitivities to work with. The wise-women share this story for I value their knowing, the pungent tea and angel-card shuffles. I expand each time with them though I offer nothing—am I lesser, incomplete? Merlin accepts and loves an owl, his companion on long nights. When shall I accept my messy value?

How Can I Belong Anywhere

sliding my gaze to hold worthy delusions;
blind to the horrors that beg me to love them?

Pterodactyls screech over two bulldog cannonballs;
Birdman fronts a stone angel with fangs.
They're gatekeeping Grief, stored in this shot iris,
keen to writhe out a kelp monster for salve as
a smile in the mirror.

A rubbery red man,
a hurricane laugh,
an axe-headed soldier's
counterpart corpse and its cavernous stare,
eave-sized eagles twitch scissor-beak gawks,
eerie crocodiles raft to the gamut of hexing fixed orbs
watching me watching me
watching me crawl,
clapping, jabbing their eyes on my form.

The soldier extends a smooth oaken heft,
the dream coach accepts

a gummy red hug. Bulldogs fed,
I try respect with high fives down the aisle,
each crack of the palm a new grounding acquired.

Mania drops for a steadier stride
so earthed shall I, feather-souled, abide.

Tentacles

Lulled by the shushing waves, we enjoy the airy caress of the dark purple sky. The silhouette of the island smoulders occasionally with distant fires hissing down Pele's braids. I draw peace into my lungs. My daughter does the same, capped with a snore. Brine smacks light kisses on the jetty pylons paddled with the under-echo; all recedes to a hum before I slip into the void, about to roam the giggling stars above.

A wrong note brings me back. The slosh is heavier, becoming more discrete; the slap... slap... slap of wet feet. I am up.
Her dad, a sprawling zombie, dries out on the jetty, exhausted. It took a lot for him to get out. I grudge him some respect.
I stand over him, "Are you okay?" but no answer. Two sleeping bodies now share this stretch of jetty. The sea is rhythmic as before; I smell only salt on the wind.
But my gut clenches; I slink to the wooden edge, body a tuned satellite dish, each fine hair a raised antenna. A

murky shape, with a mass of limbs in the water, calls me by name.

"It's you", I say, peering at the shadow filled with the faces and tethered arms of extended family. The adults grasp onto struggling youth as buoys. The chill off a smile skins the wash to blade my belly.
The head's eyes glitter. "Why don't you join us?" she says. "Her cousins would love to... *play...* with her".

My daughter had woken and tip-toed behind me. In response, she readies to jump. I grab a fistful of her shirt. "No! Just watch." I can already see her eyes, helpless then empty, under the drag.
Hmm. "Why don't you get dry up here, instead of half-drowning there?" I ask.
"We're fine, dear. We don't need the jetty."
I take a deep breath in, force the words out between teeth pretending a smile. "What about you?" I ask the cousins.
"They're fine, dear. We *like* it here. They *like* being with their *family*."
Its main body extends; multiplying arms and eyes. The moon nods on the surface of the shrugging tide; and

staring down I am pulled towards the ocean's hypnotic sway.

"Why can't I go in, Mum?" My darling girl reels me back. The creature's extremities curl around the front pylons.
"Sweetie, do you remember the black rock? The two different sides? You'll always have choices up here. And it's ok to change your mind. That's why."

We watch fresh lava pouring new land. We watch the tide creep forward and back, plucking a harvest of olivine from black sand, eroding the island slower than its forming. The lapping metronome spells an inevitable sun. One has deserted. Dawning light will loosen more bonds.

After We Cleaved

"Out beyond ideas of wrongdoing and rightdoing there is a field. I'll meet you there."
Maulana Jalal Al-Din Rumi

Eyeing splinters,
she weathers the spousal snarl:
their pet punishment
indulged for decades,
both sure she deserves it.

"Believe me, the adults cry as well,"
says Coach while I point out a child overwhelmed
on the Jiu-Jitsu mat,
"when they won't tap out of the trap."
It seems we fold down freedom, we Houdinis,
bent on figuring victory, until wedged in the ring
unwitting.

No wrong move lessens your worthiness,
runs my sundered enlightening.
When will she slip
the k/not?

Superpower

Breaking up with girlfriends is Trev's habit. He doubts his and their judgement, wonders if he might stand someone longer than a year, begs a Higher Power. Shaz interrupts:

higher-ups power-tripped on me, bluffed as we were by position, in every new job. I shifted on watching my paralysis, hoping for approval from these proxy parents. Yet they too had growing pains, exposing hubris their managers ripped through. Withstanding politics can callous or flay skin. I shed the pattern of nervous newcoming, finding it attracts a superior's ache for power; my achilles but also theirs. I was their mirror—an unresolved insecurity, they my hungry foreshadow.

We are not victims, Trev. Realise the teaching we pay to convey, and we'll end or enjoy it. The challenge is seeing our superpower.

Black Sheep Ballade

I try my best to get along
and common ground is best for interplay.
I'll smile if some are resolutely wrong;
cajole a mood that's resolutely grey
though latterly I see with some dismay
we may be resolutely out of sync.
Now sunk, I should have realised yesterday
I will not sway them to the way I think.

Why beat my head on their headstrong
insistence our grim status quo must stay?
When simply: I am round to their oblong;
my views are too outrageous to convey;
my thoughts are not their business anyway
although I'm sure our feelings interlink
for doubtless in frustration they inveigh:
"I will not sway them to the way I think!"

I won't get validation from this throng;
I know my plans, my past, my style of play;
I've simply other places I belong;
let they do them and I'll do me my way.

Self-worth is self-permission self's okay
despite the hopes of those want self to sink—
their thoughts are not my business anyway:
I will not sway them to the way I think.

Love: time and strength and breath are best to lay
at silent efforts for my groove and kink.
The step to joy is knowing that today
I will not sway them to the way I think.

Table

What do you cost me?
Are you worth the exchange?
My partner is rapt about you.
I allow his indulgence

but eschew your carved opulence,
even at home.

ii. Children

      rebel
against the refrain
You-Can't-Afford-That
sung so many times, so many chords
tighten our throats, constrict our fun
warped to a malignant grudge.

"You can't afford that",
I parrot my mother,
garrotting my partner.

"You can't afford that",
recoils his father,
evoking the pattern of Nots
to swallow at a cheaper table.

Free will is a bargain
at a few extra noughts.

iii. Homestay

I'm in the same small town
with the same view in the room and out,
the same instant coffee,
the same me but I am
taken on a magic table-ride
to sweet sixteen
billeted to a family of five
in Toulouse.

Except
their table was more medieval,
I was more primeval
and the family was more uncivil.

Such a wonderful trip
every time I sit
at la table.

iv. Relativity

The table sprawls silky knots and chalcedony.
You stroke its smooth hedonism
sized against your start-up funds.

I brace in your shock but how to say
this table demands owning my choices
unapologetic to envy.
I've learned discretion but must I be less?
Can you enjoy this
though I have it?
We're not competing for tables or business.

Rather, I ask
Where may we catch up
next time?

v. Pleasure

I can't get you off this table
You're getting more out of it than me
You know I was right about this table
my partner says.
I'm silent
smirking and laughing inside
which he takes for assent
of his unending rightness.
Thanks for this table, I love it.

Now please go away,
you're interrupting.

Naga Uta: Observance

Chef, keeping vigil
between his kitchen duties,
by the serving-hatch
would look upon the faithful.

He, one slow Tuesday
at table, blesstowed upon
a regular: chai,
eggs benedict a-vessel,
open palms and wrists
left graven on the mind
as offering then
before *thank you* he'd withdrawn
in dedication
to the cookhouse's calling
to communion with his craft.

Thank you, Softball Dad

I'd warm up a good story—swing three bats at once—
then bring doubt to the plate, pop a safe bunt
to make first and if I did it was just luck
and if I didn't it was just.

Lizzy's dad said "You'll hit a home run today"
face up, confirming truth with the sky
as my feet schlepped past him
to the weekly sentencing.

I posed with the bat—*how does he know?*
scanning, blank, suspended—
then stepped into the ball,
cracked it out to right field
and chased the team home.

I hope our riot rewarded Lizzy's dad;
I never thanked him for his kindness
thinking he was psychic;
pitching more faith in him
than myself.

Approximate Pentina

I walk a row of gorgeous houses; count
the difference of my own
lone prospects & those blessing
the possessors—none
of whom I know or know my business.

After some egregious family business
I count
along the ranking order. None
or few readily own
that painful blessing

of judgement: contempt for the black sheep is a blessing
for its freedom; its business
only to own
its future as self-approval counts
more than approval from any (which is none).

Yet there seems no sympathy, none!
for the golden child: all are entranced by blessings
bestowed count-

less terms on that fatted calf, whose business
begs jumping through hoops not its own.

I walk a row of gorgeous houses I don't own
that cost me none.
I skirt the jealous business
of tallying others' blessings.
The balance, I reckon, is unfeasible to count.

I must count my own blessings,
these houses are none of my business.

Andromeda

Light streams and spreads through every cell: softening the jaw, slackening my spine, smoothing the heart and reducing thought to a blip.

Stop! I say without sound, scattering words through the field, seeding ripples in the light. *If this is my Near Death Experience, I want to have a good one. I want to see a bit of the Universe, thanks.*

My winged guide entifies from white noise. I press myself into its shaggy neck to alight from this dimension, called by my hidden guilt to Andromeda Galaxy, the landing place I'd sent all negative energy cleansed off myself. Grey whirlwinds collecting wisps of psychic dross and blocks to energy flow: I'd flung them at the heart of Andromeda. I've been a deadbeat dumper. Now I can know the consequences.

The spiral galaxy is the Milky Way's nearest neighbor and more than double the size, 2.5 million light years from Earth and visible from home as nebulous smear.

In the light-suffused Oneness, moving through dimensions like a mirror maze of unrecognizable self-images, Andromeda is a whirling octopus; a multi-ringed eye; a yawning, angular, teeth-rimmed mouth around bright tonsils. I'd been eaten before by a cosmic octopus: my head caught by a sucker and pulled sadlong up into the salty, midnight maw. I'd emerged from its eye at Osaka's Kuromon market, handing money the next instant for tako tamago—chewy, candied, red baby octopus stuffed with a quail's egg, served on a stick. It was the reward for my devouring, our merging. I could cry to think of it now, the life gone from the egg. Where could the baby be?

The spiral galaxy glows; flashes travel along its arms. I hear reversing beacons. I stand inside a white warehouse of bright, polished concrete squeaking of forklifts and pallet jacks. The place is a giant postal service, moving light-wrapped shapes from chute to shipper.
My guilt was redundant. Matter sent here is redirected. How on Earth did I know to send stuff here?! Earth... I remember fielding wrong numbers, couriers sent to my house instead of next door, unclaimed mail I returned to

sender, many strangers to whom I'd given directions, no odd socks in my laundry.
Some parcels have the same send and return addresses—the guide intuits to me, in response to the observation, that energy changes with each redirection before suiting the place it belongs. Ah, I marvel, and recall the mirror maze. How many reflections will I reject before accepting they are all me?

Okay, I telepathize, I want to feel belonging, I want connection. For answer we are backwards in time, forward to the edge of the universe, there dissolving into superheated quark stew. I see the guide caught sideways, an awkward foreleg and hoof stuck out before rendered to fizz by the sparking, colliding mass around us.

I feel no pain, there is no I.
There is no edge but Now, This, expanding, All: the subatomic churn to build worlds and systems inside a seething ring trying to uncordon itself, racing away from the bounds that it is.

Embracing Life after Four Months of Bronchitis

Air homes in breath,
hugs these lungs; embosomed
we hold.

I squeeze back, hale
then billow afresh
this whole.

Waiting

"Dear girl, you'll never know what tears are, until you lose a child......"
Joan Walsh-Smith (September 2012) whose grandmother's words were the inspiration for her sculpture The Waiting Woman, Geraldton, Western Australia

Great-Grandma drops
tears into DNA;
washed loss through our line.

Her husband has daughters
rely on no man:
bloody wartimes.

They tinker, tailor, pilot, sail. They're
independent though
lesser for lost brothers;

generations of girls
who find power, strength
then revert to husbands,

favor ranks of men, boys,
initiate files of invisible women,
resentful ghosts

hand down festered grief,
bequeath emotional
dis-ease.

I pray: in light
await families,
sons for lost women: "We're home, Mum."

I feel weeping cleanse,
doubled
in reunion.

Letting Go of Dad

I discover we are never alone
on the 33rd anniversary
of his heart attack:

I embody a story
that survives him,
studying a subject hard to swallow:
Teaching for me
Engineering for him.

My parotid glands swell,
overwhelmed by a mentor's negativity,
exploding by the jugular.

In this lineal suffering
are we close, Dad?
Did you bleed Yes
against your inner friend,
like I'm doing now,
slaving for approval?

He says nothing;
he is only a weight
in my chest; an angry beat
that dares leak a single note
resisting

my narcissist's self-image
and hopes she'll prop mine.
I am fired,
failed.
Dad,

is this is how you felt—
damaged, relieved, free?

Can you go?

Are you there?

ii. An Old Haunt

Time walls a well
yet still
open on a warm, dark mourning
to commune with you.

I wring libations from hot springs,
seek oblivion in the plunge-pool
lured by undiscovered bedrock.
The abyss is proof
of fathomless love.

I break for air
puffy   pale   clean.

iii. Three's a-Proud

All Pommies are bastards!
sang Dad about Grandpa;
voice ringing with glee,
rebellion, grief;
the refrains slinging rounds

of expectation unmet,
disappointment resented,
back to a distant patriarch.

Dad would never know
but I saw, every visit
after the funeral,
Grandpa wish silence undone
with his wretched son
who junked a future on the army,
wasting talent—that bright,
baby boy.

They're having a beer now,
spiffy in uniform:
WW2 and Vietnam.
Keep one chilled for me boys,
I'll join you in mess dress
and laugh last of tragic parents
when I'm done down here.

Rebirth

rolling to crawling to tottering gait
shunting along she must carry this weight
onward momentum with clearing our freight
thunders us forward to switch the line's fate
teaching the heart is the trainer now eight
this is my track it is long it is straight

www.ingramcontent.com/pod-product-compliance
Lightning Source LLC
Chambersburg PA
CBHW051956290426
44110CB00015B/2266